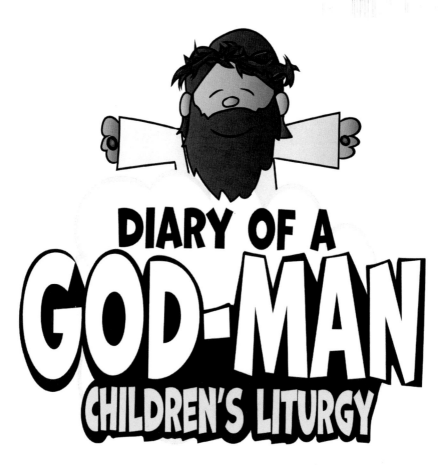

DIARY OF A GOD-MAN
CHILDREN'S LITURGY

created by kids for kids

TREATY OAK PUBLISHERS

PUBLISHER'S NOTE

This is a work of personal inspiration.

Excerpts from the *Lectionary for Mass for Use in the Dioceses of the United States of America, second typical edition* © 2001, 1998, 1997, 1986, 1970 Confraternity of Christian Doctrine, Inc., Washington, D.C. Used with permission. All rights reserved. No portion of this text may be reproduced by any means without permission in writing from the copyright owner.

Link to website and other info:
www.diaryofagodman.com
godman82020@gmail.com
@diary_of_a_godman - Instagram
@DiaryofaGodMan - Facebook

Printed and published in the United States of America

TREATY OAK PUBLISHERS

ISBN-978-1-943658-57-2

Available in print and digital from Amazon

A Spanish language version is also available

DEDICATION

This book is dedicated to Jesus, Mary, and Joseph
and to families all over the world.

"As the family goes, so goes the nation and so goes the whole world
in which we live."

Saint John Paul the Great (Pope John Paul II)

TABLE OF CONTENTS

ADVENT

CHRISTMAS

ORDINARY TIME

TESTIMONIALS

My kids and I look forward to these every week! Thank you and congrats on the first Misalette! Enid

My sons (ages 11, 7, 4) are loving these! Thank you for sharing! Melissa

These are perfect for my children's catechism. Brianne

I love these! Sharing with my kids today. Laura

Will you post your website? My kids would love using these every week. Amanda

They are beautiful. Thank you so much! Miriana

Amazing! My kids think these are so cool! Lisa

These will be so helpful for our children! Thank you so much. May God bless your project. Monica

Great idea to keep the kids interested in going to mass. God bless. Wendy

These are brilliant! Lizzy

Can't wait to show my kids. They are big Dogman fans, so this is right up their alley. Laura

DIARY OF A GOD-MAN CHARACTERS

God the Father

God the Son

God the Holy Spirit

Aaron

Aaron's Sons

Adam

Andrew

Anna

David

Devil

Eli

Elizabeth

Eve

Gabriel

Herod

Isaiah

John

John the Baptist

Jonah

Joseph　　Joshua　　Magi　　Mary

Moses　　Nathan　　Paul　　Peter

Samuel　　Saul　　Shepherds　　Simeon

ADVENT

FIRST SUNDAY OF ADVENT

ISAIAH 1ST READING 63:16B-17, 19B; 64:2-7

You, LORD, are our father, / our redeemer you are named forever. / Why do you let us wander, O LORD, from your ways, / and harden our hearts so that we fear you not? / Return for the sake of your servants, the tribes of your heritage. / Oh, that you would rend the heavens and come down, / with the mountains quaking before you, / while you wrought awesome deeds we could not hope for, / such as they had not heard of from of old. /

No ear has ever heard, no eye ever seen, any God but you / doing such deeds for those who wait for him. / Would that you might meet us doing right, / that we were mindful of you in our ways! / Behold, you are angry, and we are sinful; / all of us have become like unclean people, / all our good deeds are like polluted rags; / we have all withered like leaves, / and our guilt carries us away like the wind.

There is none who calls upon your name, / who rouses himself to cling to you; / for you have hidden your face from us / and have delivered us up to our guilt. / Yet, O LORD, you are our father; / we are the clay and you the potter: / we are all the work of your hands.

PSALM
80:2-3, 15-16, 18-19

O shepherd of Israel, hearken,
from your throne upon the cherubim, shine forth.
Rouse your power,
and come to save us.

LORD, MAKE US TURN TO YOU;
LET US SEE YOUR FACE AND WE
SHALL BE SAVED

Once again, O LORD of hosts,
look down from heaven, and see;
take care of this vine,
and protect what your right hand has planted
the son of man whom you yourself made strong.

May your help be with the man of your right hand,
with the son of man whom you yourself made strong.
Then we will no more withdraw from you;
give us new life, and we will call upon your name.

2ND READING

1 CORINTHIANS 1:3-9

Brothers and sisters: Grace to you and peace from God our Father and the Lord Jesus Christ.

I give thanks to my God always on your account for the grace of God bestowed on you in Christ Jesus, that in him you were enriched in every way, with all discourse and all knowledge, as the testimony to Christ was confirmed among you, so that you are not lacking in any spiritual gift as you wait for the revelation of our Lord Jesus Christ. He will keep you firm to the end, irreproachable on the day of our Lord Jesus Christ. God is faithful, and by him you were called to fellowship with his Son, Jesus Christ our Lord.

GOSPEL MARK 13:33-37

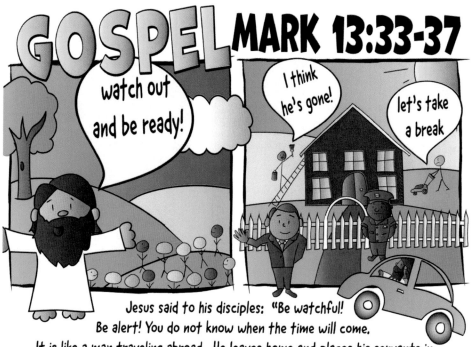

Jesus said to his disciples: "Be watchful! Be alert! You do not know when the time will come. It is like a man traveling abroad. He leaves home and places his servants in charge, – each with his own work, and orders the gatekeeper to be on the watch. Watch, therefore; you do not know when the Lord of the house is coming, whether in the evening, or at midnight, or at cockcrow, or in the morning. May he not come suddenly and find you sleeping. What I say to you, I say to all: ' Watch!'"

SECOND SUNDAY OF ADVENT
1ST READING
ISAIAH 40:1-5, 9-11

Comfort, give comfort to my people, / says your God. / Speak tenderly to Jerusalem, and proclaim to her / that her service is at an end, / her guilt is expiated; / indeed, she has received from the hand of the LORD / double for all her sins.

A voice cries out: / In the desert prepare the way of the LORD! / Make straight in the wasteland a highway for our God! / Every valley shall be filled in, / every mountain and hill shall be made low; / the rugged land shall be made a plain, / the rough country, a broad valley. / Then the glory of the LORD shall be revealed, / and all people shall see it together; / for the mouth of the LORD has spoken.

Go up on to a high mountain, / Zion, herald of glad tidings; / cry out at the top of your voice, / Jerusalem, herald of good news! / Fear not to cry out / and say to the cities of Judah: / Here is your God! / Here comes with power / the Lord GOD, / who rules by his strong arm; / here is his reward with him, / his recompense before him. / Like a shepherd he feeds his flock; / in his arms he gathers the lambs, / carrying them in his bosom, / and leading the ewes with care.

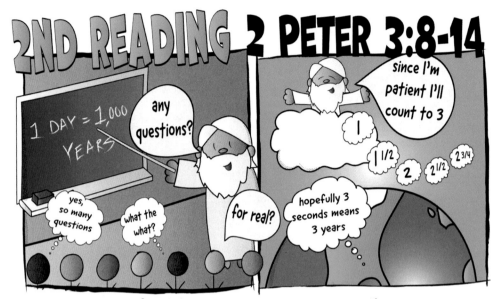

Do not ignore this one fact, beloved, that with the Lord one day is like a thousand years and a thousand years like one day. The Lord does not delay his promise, as some regard "delay," but he is patient with you, not wishing that any should perish but that all should come to repentance. But the day of the Lord will come like a thief, and then the heavens will pass away with a mighty roar and the elements will be dissolved by fire, and the earth and everything done on it will be found out.

Since everything is to be dissolved in this way, what sort of persons ought you to be, conducting yourselves in holiness and devotion, waiting for and hastening the coming of the day of God, because of which the heavens will be dissolved in flames and the elements melted by fire. But according to his promise we await new heavens and a new earth in which righteousness dwells. Therefore, beloved, since you await these things, be eager to be found without spot or blemish before him, at peace.

The beginning of the gospel of Jesus Christ the Son of God.
As it is written in Isaiah the prophet:
   Behold, I am sending my messenger ahead of you;
      he will prepare your way.
   A voice of one crying out in the desert:
      "Prepare the way of the Lord,
   make straight his paths."

GOSPEL
MARK 1:1-8

John the Baptist appeared in the desert proclaiming a baptism of repentance for the forgiveness of sins.

People of the whole Judean countryside
and all the inhabitants of Jerusalem were going out to him and were being
baptized by him in the Jordan Riveras they acknowledged their sins. John was
clothed in camel's hair with a leather belt around his waist. He fed on locusts
and wild honey. And this is what he proclaimed: "One mightier than I is coming
after me.I am not worthy to stoop and loosen the thongs of his sandals. I have
baptized you with water; he will baptize you with the Holy Spirit."

After the man, Adam, had eaten of the tree, the LORD God called to the man and asked him, "Where are you?" He answered, "I heard you in the garden; but I was afraid, because I was naked, so I hid myself."

Then he asked, "Who told you that you were naked? You have eaten, then, from the tree of which I had forbidden you to eat!" The man replied, "The woman whom you put here with me she gave me fruit from the tree, and so I ate it. The LORD God then asked the woman, "Why did you do such a thing?" The woman answered, "The serpent tricked me into it, so I ate it."

Then the LORD God said to the serpent: / "Because you have done this, you shall be banned / from all the animals / and from all the wild creatures; / on your belly shall you crawl, / and dirt shall you eat / all the days of your life. / I will put enmity between you and the woman, / and between your offspring and hers; / he will strike at your head, while you strike at his heel." / The man called his wife Eve, because she became the mother of all the living.

PSALM
98:1, 2-3AB, 3CD-4

Sing to the LORD a new song,
for he has done wondrous deeds;
His right hand has won victory for him,
his holy arm.

The LORD has made his salvation known:
in the sight of the nations he has revealed his justice.
He has remembered his kindness and his faithfulness
toward the house of Israel.

All the ends of the earth have seen
the salvation by our God.
Sing joyfully to the LORD, all you lands;
break into song; sing praise.

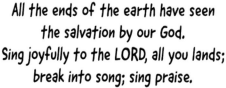

SING TO THE LORD
A NEW SONG, FOR HE HAS
DONE MARVELOUS DEEDS.

Brothers and sisters: Blessed be the God and Father of our Lord Jesus Christ, who has blessed us in Christ with every spiritual blessing in the heavens, as he chose us in him, before the foundation of the world, to be holy and without blemish before him.

In love he destined us for adoption to himself through Jesus Christ, in accord with the favor of his will, for the praise of the glory of his grace that he granted us in the beloved.

In him we were also chosen, destined in accord with the purpose of the One who accomplishes all things according to the intention of his will, so that we might exist for the praise of his glory, we who first hoped in Christ.

The angel Gabriel was sent from God to a town of Galilee called Nazareth, to a virgin betrothed to a man named Joseph, of the house of David, and the virgin's name was Mary. And coming to her, he said, "Hail, full of grace! The Lord is with you." But she was greatly troubled at what was said and pondered what sort of greeting this might be. Then the angel said to her, "Do not be afraid, Mary, for you have found favor with God. Behold, you will conceive in your womb and bear a son, and you shall name him Jesus. He will be great and will be called Son of the Most High, and the Lord God will give him the throne of David his father, and he will rule over the house of Jacob forever, and of his Kingdom there will be no end."

But Mary said to the angel, "How can this be, since I have no relations with a man?" And the angel said to her in reply, "The Holy Spirit will come upon you, and the power of the Most High will overshadow you. Therefore the child to be born will be called holy, the Son of God. And behold, Elizabeth, your relative, has also conceived a son in her old age, and this is the sixth month for her who was called barren; for nothing will be impossible for God." Mary said, "Behold, I am the handmaid of the Lord. May it be done to me according to your word." Then the angel departed from her.

The spirit of the Lord GOD is upon me, / because the LORD has anointed me; / he has sent me to bring glad tidings to the poor, / to heal the brokenhearted, / to proclaim liberty to the captives / and release to the prisoners, / to announce a year of favor from the LORD / and a day of vindication by our God.

I rejoice heartily in the LORD, / in my God is the joy of my soul; / for he has clothed me with a robe of salvation / and wrapped me in a mantle of justice, / like a bridegroom adorned with a diadem, / like a bride bedecked with her jewels. / As the earth brings forth its plants, / and a garden makes its growth spring up, / so will the Lord GOD make justice and praise / spring up before all the nations.

THIRD SUNDAY OF ADVENT 1ST READING
ISAIAH 61:1-2A, 10-11

PSALM
LK 1:46-48, 49-50, 53-54

My soul proclaims the greatness of the Lord;
my spirit rejoices in God my Savior,
for he has looked upon his lowly servant.
From this day all generations will call me blessed:

MY SOUL REJOICES IN MY GOD

ISHMAEL ABRAHAM ISAAC REBEKAH
HAGAR SARAH JACOB ESAU
DAVID
RACHEL ZILPAH
LEAH JOSEPH MARY

FAMILY TREE

JESUS

the Almighty has done great things for me,
and holy is his Name.
He has mercy on those who fear him
in every generation.

He has filled the hungry with good things,
and the rich he has sent away empty.
He has come to the help of his servant Israel
for he has remembered his promise of mercy,

2ND READING 1 THESSALONIANS 5:16-24

Rejoice always. Pray without ceasing. In all circumstances give thanks, for this is the will of God for you in Christ Jesus. Do not quench the Spirit. Do not despise prophetic utterances. Test everything; retain what is good. Refrain from every kind of evil.

May the God of peace make you perfectly holy and may you entirely, spirit, soul, and body, be preserved blameless for the coming of our Lord Jesus Christ. The one who calls you is faithful, and he will also accomplish it.

GOSPEL
JOHN 1:6-8, 19-28

A man named John was sent from God. He came for testimony, to testify to the light, so that all might believe through him. He was not the light, but came to testify to the light.

And this is the testimony of John. When the Jews from Jerusalem sent priests and Levites to him to ask him, "Who are you?" He admitted and did not deny it, but admitted, "I am not the Christ." So they asked him, "What are you then? Are you Elijah?" And he said, "I am not." "Are you the Prophet?" He answered, "No." So they said to him, "Who are you, so we can give an answer to those who sent us? What do you have to say for yourself?"

He said:
"I am the voice of one crying out in the desert, 'make straight the way of the Lord,'"

as Isiah the prophet said." Some Pharisees were also sent. They asked him, "Why then do you baptize if you are not the Christ or Elijah or the Prophet?" John answered them, "I baptize with water; but there is one among you whom you do not recnogize, the one who is coming after me, whose sandle strap I am not worthy to untie." This happened in Bethany across the Jordan, where John was baptizing.

FOURTH SUNDAY OF ADVENT

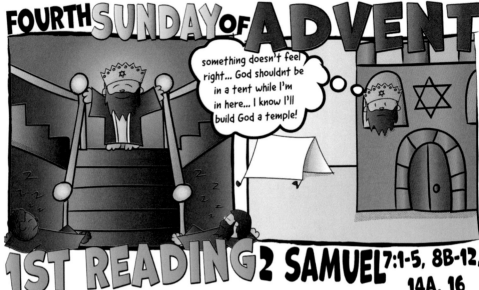

1ST READING 2 SAMUEL 7:1-5, 8B-12, 14A, 16

When King David was settled in his palace, and the LORD had given him rest from his enemies on every side, he said to Nathan the prophet, "Here I am living in a house of cedar, while the ark of God dwells in a tent!" Nathan answered the king, "Go, do whatever you have in mind, for the LORD is with you." But that night the LORD spoke to Nathan and said: "Go, tell my servant David, ' Thus says the LORD: Should you build me a house to dwell in?

'" It was I who took you from the pasture and from the care of the flock to be commander of my people Israel. I have been with you wherever you went, and I have destroyed all your enemies before you. And I will make you famous like the great ones of the earth.

I will fix a place for my people Israel; I will plant them so that they may dwell in their place without further disturbance. Neither shall the wicked continue to afflict them as they did of old, since the time I first appointed judges over my people Israel. I will give you rest from all your enemies. The LORD also reveals to you that he will establish a house for you. And when your time comes and you rest with your ancestors, I will raise up your heir after you, sprung from your loins, and I will make his kingdom firm. I will be a father to him, and he shall be a son to me. Your house and your kingdom shall endure forever before me; your throne shall stand firm forever.'"

2ND READING ROMANS 16:25-27

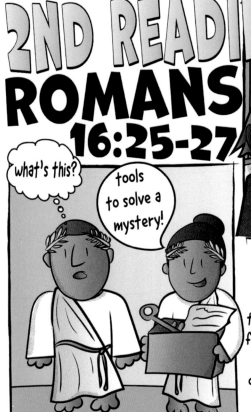

Brothers and sisters: To him who can strengthen you, according to my gospel and the proclamation of Jesus Christ, according to the revelation of the mystery kept secret for long ages but now manifested through the prophetic writings and, according to he command of the eternal God, made known to all nations to bring about the obedience of faith, to the only wise God, through Jesus Christ be glory forever and ever. Amen.

LUKE 1:26-38

The angel Gabriel was sent from God to a town of Galilee called Nazareth, to a virgin betrothed to a man named Joseph, of the house of David, and the virgin's name was Mary. And coming to her, he said, "Hail, full of grace! The Lord is with you." But she was greatly troubled at what was said and pondered what sort of greeting this might be. Then the angel said to her, "Do not be afraid, Mary, for you have found favor with God.

"Behold, you will conceive in your womb and bear a son, and you shall name him Jesus. He will be great and will be called Son of the Most High, and the Lord God will give him the throne of David his father, and he will rule over the house of Jacob forever, and of his kingdom there will be no end."

But Mary said to the angel, "How can this be, since I have no relations with a man?" And the angel said to her in reply, "The Holy Spirit will come upon you, and the power of the Most High will overshadow you. Therefore the child to be born will be called holy, the Son of God. And behold, Elizabeth, your relative, has also conceived a son in her old age, and this is the sixth month for her who was called barren; for nothing will be impossible for God." Mary said, "Behold, I am the handmaid of the Lord. May it be done to me according to your word." Then the angel departed from her.

CHRISTMAS

CHRISTMAS VIGIL MASS
1ST READING ISAIAH 62:1-5
(other readings may be chosen)

For Zion's sake I will not be silent, / for Jerusalem's sake I will not be quiet, / until her vindication shines forth like the dawn / and her victory like a burning torch. /

Nations shall behold your vindication, / and all the kings your glory; / you shall be called by a new name / pronounced by the mouth of the LORD. / You shall be a glorious crown in the hand of the LORD, / a royal diadem held by your God. /

No more shall people call you "Forsaken," / or your land "Desolate," / but you shall be called "My Delight," / and your land "Espoused." / For the LORD delights in you / and makes your land his spouse. / As a young man marries a virgin, / your Builder shall marry you; / and as a bridegroom rejoices in his bride / so shall your God rejoice in you.

When Paul reached Antioch in Pisidia and entered the synagogue, he stood up, motioned with his hand, and said, "Fellow Israelites and you others who are God-fearing, listen. The God of this people Israel chose our ancestors and exalted the people during their sojourn in the land of Egypt.

2ND READING ACTS 13:16-17, 22-25

With uplifted arm he led them out of it. Then he removed Saul and raised up David as king; of him he testified, 'I have found David, son of Jesse, a man after my own heart; he will carry out my every wish.' From this man's descendants God, according to his promise, has brought to Israel a savior, Jesus. John heralded his coming by proclaiming a baptism of repentance to all the people of Israel; and as John was completing his course, he would say,' What do you suppose that I am? I am not he. Behold, one is coming after me; I am not worthy to unfasten the sandals of his feet.'"

GOSPEL MATTHEW 1:18-25
(Longer option may be chosen)

This is how the birth of Jesus Christ came about. When his mother Mary was betrothed to Joseph, but before they lived together, she was found with child through the Holy Spirit. Joseph her husband, since he was a righteous man, yet unwilling to expose her to shame, decided to divorce her quietly. Such was his intention when, behold, the angel of the Lord appeared to him in a dream and said, "Joseph, son of David, do not be afraid to take Mary your wife into your home. For it is through the Holy Spirit that this child has been conceived in her.

She will bear a son and you are to name him Jesus, because he will save his people from their sins." All this took place to fulfill what the Lord had said through the prophet: Behold, the virgin shall conceive and bear a son, / and they shall name him Emmanuel, which means "God is with us." When Joseph awoke, he did as the angel of the Lord had commanded him and took his wife into his home. He had no relations with her until she bore a son, and he named him Jesus.

THE HOLY FAMILY OF JESUS MARY AND JOSEPH

1ST READING SIRACH 3:2-6, 12-14

(OTHER READINGS MAY BE CHOSEN)

God sets a father in honor over his children; / a mother's authority he confirms over her sons. / Whoever honors his father atones for sins, / and preserves himself from them. / When he prays, he is heard; / he stores up riches who reveres his mother. / Whoever honors his father is gladdened by children, / and, when he prays, is heard. / Whoever reveres his father will live a long life; / he who obeys his father brings comfort to his mother. /

My son, take care of your father when he is old; / grieve him not as long as he lives. / Even if his mind fail, be considerate of him; / revile him not all the days of his life; / kindness to a father will not be forgotten, / firmly planted against the debt of your sins / —a house raised in justice to you.

PSALM
128:1-2, 3, 4-5

Blessed is everyone who fears the LORD,
who walks in his ways!
For you shall eat the fruit of your handiwork;
blessed shall you be, and favored.

Your wife shall be like a fruitful vine
in the recesses of your home;
your children like olive plants
around your table.

BLESSED ARE THOSE WHO FEAR THE LORD AND WALK IN HIS WAYS

Behold, thus is the man blessed
who fears the LORD.
The LORD bless you from Zion:
may you see the prosperity of Jerusalem
all the days of your life.

2ND READING COLOSSIANS 3:12-17
(Longer option may be chosen)

Brothers and sisters: Put on, as God's chosen ones, holy and beloved, heartfelt compassion, kindness, humility, gentleness, and patience, bearing with one another and forgiving one another, if one has a grievance against another; as the Lord has forgiven you, so must you also do. And over all these put on love, that is, the bond of perfection. And let the peace of Christ control your hearts, the peace into which you were also called in one body.

And be thankful. Let the word of Christ dwell in you richly, as in all wisdom you teach and admonish one another, singing psalms, hymns, and spiritual songs with gratitude in your hearts to God. And whatever you do, in word or in deed, do everything in the name of the Lord Jesus, giving thanks to God the Father through him.

GOSPEL

LUKE 2:22-40
(Shorter option may be chosen)

When the days were completed for their purification according to the law of Moses, They took him up to Jerusalem to present him to the Lord, just as it is written in the law of the Lord, *Every male that opens the womb shall be consecrated to the Lord*, and to offer the sacrifice of *a pair of turtledoves or two young pigeons*, in accordance with the dictate in the law of the Lord.

Now there was a man in Jerusalem whose name was Simeon. This man was righteous and devout, awaiting the consolation of Israel, and the Holy Spirit was upon him. It had been revealed to him by the Holy Spirit that he should not see death before he had seen the Christ of the Lord.

He came in the Spirit into the temple; and when the parents brought in the child Jesus to perform the custom of the law in regard to him, He took him into his arms and blessed God, saying: "Now, Master, you may let your servant go / in peace, according to your word, / for my eyes have seen your salvation, / which you prepared in sight of all the peoples, / a light for revelation to the Gentiles, / and glory for your people Israel." The child's father and mother were amazed at what was said about him; and Simeon blessed them and said to Mary his mother, "Behold, this child is destined for the fall and rise of many in Israel, and to be a sign that will be contradicted —and you yourself a sword will pierce— so that the thoughts of many hearts may be revealed." There was also a prophetess, Anna, the daughter of Phanuel, of the tribe of Asher. She was advanced in years, having lived seven years with her husband after her marriage, and then as a widow until she was eighty-four. She never left the temple, but worshiped night and day with fasting and prayer. And coming forward at that very time, she gave thanks to God and spoke about the child to all who were awaiting the redemption of Jerusalem.

When they had fulfilled all the prescriptions of the law of the Lord, they returned to Galilee, to their own town of Nazareth. The child grew and became strong, filled with wisdom; and the favor of God was upon him.

THE SOLEMNITY OF MARY MOTHER OF GOD

1ST READING NUMBERS 6:22–27

The LORD said to Moses: "Speak to Aaron and his sons and tell them: This is how you shall bless the Israelites. Say to them:

The LORD bless you and keep you! / The LORD let his face shine upon you, and be gracious to you! / The LORD look upon you kindly and give you peace! / So shall they invoke my name upon the Israelites, and I will bless them."

MAY GOD BLESS US IN HIS MERCY

PSALM 67:2-3, 5, 6, 8

May God have pity on us and bless us;
may he let his face shine upon us.
So may your way be known upon earth;
among all nations, your salvation.

May the nations be glad and exult
because you rule the peoples in equity;
the nations on the earth you guide.

May the peoples praise you, O God;
may all the peoples praise you!
May God bless us,
and may all the ends of the earth fear him!

2ND READING GALATIANS 4:4-7

Brothers and sisters: When the fullness of time had come, God sent his Son,
born of a woman, born under the law, to ransom those under the law,
so that we might receive adoption as sons. As proof that you are sons,
God sent the Spirit of his Son into our hearts, crying out, "Abba, Father!"
So you are no longer a slave but a son, and if a son then also an heir, through God.

GOSPEL LUKE 2:16-21

The shepherds went in haste to Bethlehem and found Mary and Joseph, and the infant lying in the manger. When they saw this, they made known the message that had been told them about this child. All who heard it were amazed by what had been told them by the shepherds. And Mary kept all these things, reflecting on them in her heart. Then the shepherds returned, glorifying and praising God for all they had heard and seen, just as it had been told to them.

When eight days were completed for his circumcision, he was named Jesus, the name given him by the angel before he was conceived in the womb.

Rise up in splendor, Jerusalem! Your light has come, / the glory of the Lord shines upon you. / See, darkness covers the earth, / and thick clouds cover the peoples; / but upon you the LORD shines, / and over you appears his glory. / Nations shall walk by your light, / and kings by your shining radiance. / Raise your eyes and look about; / they all gather and come to you: / your sons come from afar, and your daughters in the arms of their nurses. /

THE EPIPHANY OF THE LORD
1ST READING ISAIAH 60:1-6

Then you shall be radiant at what you see, / your heart shall throb and overflow, / for the riches of the sea shall be emptied out before you, / the wealth of nations shall be brought to you. / Caravans of camels shall fill you, / dromedaries from Midian and Ephah; / all from Sheba shall come / bearing gold and frankincense, / and proclaiming the praises of the LORD.

PSALM 72:1-2, 7-8, 10-11, 12-13

O God, with your judgment endow the king,
and with your justice, the king's son;
He shall govern your people with justice
and your afflicted ones with judgment.

Justice shall flower in his days,
and profound peace, till the moon be no more.
May he rule from sea to sea,
and from the River to the ends of the earth.

LORD, EVERY NATION ON EARTH WILL ADORE YOU

The kings of Tarshish and the Isles shall offer gifts;
the kings of Arabia and Seba shall bring tribute.
All kings shall pay him homage,
all nations shall serve him.

For he shall rescue the poor when he cries out,
and the afflicted when he has no one to help him.
He shall have pity for the lowly and the poor;
the lives of the poor he shall save.

2ND READING EPHESIANS 3:2-3a, 5-6

Brothers and sisters: You have heard of the stewardship of God's grace that was given to me for your benefit, namely, that the mystery was made known to me by revelation. It was not made known to people in other generations as it has now been revealed to his holy apostles and prophets by the Spirit: that the Gentiles are coheirs, members of the same body, and copartners in the promise in Christ Jesus through the gospel.

GOSPEL
MATTHEW 2:1-12

When Jesus was born in Bethlehem of Judea, in the days of King Herod, behold, magi from the east arrived in Jerusalem, saying, "Where is the newborn king of the Jews? We saw his star at its rising and have come to do him homage." When King Herod heard this, he was greatly troubled, and all Jerusalem with him. Assembling all the chief priests and the scribes of the people, He inquired of them where the Christ was to be born. They said to him, "In Bethlehem of Judea, for thus it has been written through the prophet:

And you, Bethlehem, land of Judah,
are by no means least among the rulers of Judah;
since from you shall come a ruler,
who is to shepherd my people Israel."

Then Herod called the magi secretly and ascertained from them the time of the star's appearance. He sent them to Bethlehem and said, "Go and search diligently for the child. When you have found him, bring me word, that I too may go and do him homage. "After their audience with the king they set out. And behold, the star that they had seen at its rising preceded them, until it came and stopped over the place where the child was. They were overjoyed at seeing the star, and on entering the house they saw the child with Mary his mother. They prostrated themselves and did him homage. Then they opened their treasures and offered him gifts of gold, frankincense, and myrrh. And having been warned in a dream not to return to Herod, they departed for their country by another way.

ORDINARY TIME

1ST READING ISAIAH 42:1-4, 6-7

(Other Readings may be chosen)

Thus says the LORD:
Here is my servant whom I uphold, / my chosen one with whom
I am pleased, / upon whom I have put my spirit; / he shall bring forth justice to the
nations, / not crying out, not shouting, / not making his voice heard in the street. /
a bruised reed he shall not break, / and a smoldering wick he shall not quench, / until he
establishes justice on the earth; / the coastlands will wait for his teaching.

I, the LORD, have called you for the victory of justice, / I have grasped you by the hand;
/ I formed you, and set you / as a covenant of the people, /a light for the nations, / to
open the eyes of the blind, / to bring out prisoners from confinement, /
and from the dungeon, those who live in darkness.

PSALM
29:1-2, 3-4, 3, 9-10

Give to the LORD, you sons of God,
give to the LORD glory and praise,
Give to the LORD the glory due his name;
adore the LORD in holy attire.

THE LORD WILL BLESS HIS PEOPLE WITH PEACE

The voice of the LORD is over the waters,
the LORD, over vast waters.
The voice of the LORD is mighty;
the voice of the LORD is majestic.

The God of glory thunders,
and in his temple all say, "Glory!"
The LORD is enthroned above the flood;
the LORD is enthroned as king forever.

Peter proceeded to speak to those gathered in the house of Cornelius, saying: "In truth, I see that God shows no partiality. Rather, in every nation whoever fears him and acts uprightly is acceptable to him. You know the word that he sent to the Israelites as he proclaimed peace through Jesus Christ, who is Lord of all, what has happened all over Judea, beginning in Galilee after the baptism that John preached, how God anointed Jesus of Nazareth with the Holy Spirit and power. He went about doing good and healing all those oppressed by the devil, for God was with him."

GOSPEL MARK 1:7-11

This is what John the Baptist proclaimed: "One mightier than I is coming after me. I am not worthy to stoop and loosen the thongs of his sandals. I have baptized you with water; he will baptize you with the Holy Spirit."

It happened in those days that Jesus came from Nazareth of Galilee and was baptized in the Jordan by John. On coming up out of the water he saw the heavens being torn open and the Spirit, like a dove, descending upon him. And a voice came from the heavens, "You are my beloved Son; with you I am well pleased."

THE SECOND SUNDAY OF ORDINARY TIME

1ST READING 1 SAMUEL 3:3b–10, 19

Samuel was sleeping in the temple of the LORD where the ark of God was. The LORD called to Samuel, who answered, "Here I am." Samuel ran to Eli and said, "Here I am. You called me." "I did not call you," Eli said. "Go back to sleep." So he went back to sleep. Again the LORD called Samuel, who rose and went to Eli. "Here I am, " he said. "You called me." But Eli answered, "I did not call you, my son. Go back to sleep."

At that time Samuel was not familiar with the LORD, because the LORD had not revealed anything to him as yet. The LORD called Samuel again, for the third time. Getting up and going to Eli, he said, "Here I am. You called me." Then Eli understood that the LORD was calling the youth. So he said to Samuel, "Go to sleep, and if you are called, reply, Speak, LORD, for your servant is listening." When Samuel went to sleep in his place, the LORD came and revealed his presence, calling out as before, "Samuel, Samuel!" Samuel answered, "Speak, for your servant is listening."

Samuel grew up, and the LORD was with him, not permitting any word of his to be without effect.

40:2, 4, 7-8, 8-9, 10 PSALM

I have waited, waited for the LORD,
and he stooped toward me and heard my cry.
And he put a new song into my mouth,
a hymn to our God.

Sacrifice or offering you wished not,
but ears open to obedience you gave me.
Holocausts or sin-offerings you sought not;
then said I, "Behold I come."

♫ HERE AM I, LORD; I COME TO DO YOUR WILL

"In the written scroll it is prescribed for me
to do your will, O my God, is my delight,
and your law is within my heart!"

I announced your justice in the vast assembly;
I did not restrain my lips, as you, O LORD, know.

2ND READING 1 CORINTHIANS 6:13c-15a, 17-20

Brothers and sisters: The body is not for immorality, but for the Lord, and the Lord is for the body; God raised the Lord and will also raise us by his power.

Do you not know that your bodies are members of Christ? But whoever is joined to the Lord becomes one Spirit with him. Avoid immorality. Every other sin a person commits is outside the body, but the immoral person sins against his own body. Do you not know that your body is a temple of the Holy Spirit within you, whom you have from God, and that you are not your own? For you have been purchased at a price. Therefore glorify God in your body.

JOHN 1:35-42 GOSPEL

John was standing with two of his disciples, and as he watched Jesus walk by, he said, "Behold, the Lamb of God." The two disciples heard what he said and followed Jesus. Jesus turned and saw them following him and said to them, "What are you looking for?" They said to him, "Rabbi" — which translated means Teacher —, "where are you staying?" He said to them, "Come, and you will see." So they went and saw where Jesus was staying, and they stayed with him that day. It was about four in the afternoon. Andrew, the brother of Simon Peter, was one of the two who heard John and followed Jesus. He first found his own brother Simon and told him, "We have found the Messiah" — which is translated Christ —. Then he brought him to Jesus. Jesus looked at him and said, "You are Simon the son of John; you will be called Cephas" — which is translated Peter.

JONAH 3:1-5, 10 1ST READING

THE THIRD SUNDAY IN ORDINARY TIME

The word of the LORD came to Jonah, saying: "Set out for the great city of Nineveh, and announce to it the message that I will tell you." So Jonah made ready and went to Nineveh, according to the LORD'S bidding. Now Nineveh was an enormously large city; it took three days to go through it. Jonah began his journey through the city, and had gone but a single day's walk announcing, "Forty days more and Nineveh shall be destroyed," when the people of Nineveh believed God; they proclaimed a fast and all of them, great and small, put on sackcloth.

When God saw by their actions how they turned from their evil way, he repented of the evil that he had threatened to do to them; he did not carry it out.

PSALM
25:4-5, 6-7, 8-9

Your ways, O LORD, make known to me;
teach me your paths,
Guide me in your truth and teach me,
for you are God my savior.

TEACH ME YOUR WAYS, O LORD

I will Remember you!

proud pappa!

Remember that your compassion, O LORD,
and your love are from of old.
In your kindness remember me,
because of your goodness, O LORD.

Good and upright is the LORD;
thus he shows sinners the way.
He guides the humble to justice
and teaches the humble his way.

2ND READING 1 CORINTHIANS 7:29-31

I tell you, brothers and sisters, the time is running out. From now on, let those having wives act as not having them, those weeping as not weeping, those rejoicing as not rejoicing, those buying as not owning, those using the world as not using it fully. For the world in its present form is passing away.

GOSPEL MARK 1:14-20

After John had been arrested, Jesus came to Galilee proclaiming the gospel of God: "This is the time of fulfillment. The kingdom of God is at hand. Repent, and believe in the gospel."

As he passed by the Sea of Galilee, he saw Simon and his brother Andrew casting their nets into the sea; they were fishermen. Jesus said to them, "Come after me, and I will make you fishers of men." Then they abandoned their nets and followed him. He walked along a little farther and saw James, the son of Zebedee, and his brother John. They too were in a boat mending their nets. Then he called them. So they left their father Zebedee in the boat along with the hired men and followed him.

FOURTH SUNDAY OF ORDINARY TIME
1ST READING DEUTERONOMY 18:15-20

Moses spoke to all the people, saying: "A prophet like me will the LORD, your God, raise up for you from among your own kin; to him you shall listen. This is exactly what you requested of the LORD, your God, at Horeb on the day of the assembly, when you said, 'Let us not again hear the voice of the LORD, our God, nor see this great fire any more, lest we die.'

And the LORD said to me, 'This was well said. I will raise up for them a prophet like you from among their kin, and will put my words into his mouth; he shall tell them all that I command him. Whoever will not listen to my words which he speaks in my name, I myself will make him answer for it. But if a prophet presumes to speak in my name an oracle that I have not commanded him to speak, or speaks in the name of other gods, he shall die.'"

Come, let us sing joyfully to the LORD;
let us acclaim the rock of our salvation.
Let us come into his presence with thanksgiving;
let us joyfully sing psalms to him.

Come, let us bow down in worship;
let us kneel before the LORD who made us.
For he is our God,
and we are the people he shepherds, the flock he guides.

PSALM 95:1-2, 6-7, 7-9

NOT THIS | THIS

give me water now!

may I please have some water?

Oh, that today you would hear his voice:
"Harden not your hearts as at Meribah,
as in the day of Massah in the desert,
Where your fathers tempted me;
they tested me though they had seen my works."

IF TODAY YOU HEAR HIS VOICE, HARDEN NOT YOUR HEARTS

Brothers and sisters: I should like you to be free of anxieties. An unmarried man is anxious about the things of the Lord, how he may please the Lord. But a married man is anxious about the things of the world, how he may please his wife, and he is divided. An unmarried woman or a virgin is anxious about the things of the Lord, so that she may be holy in both body and spirit.

A married woman, on the other hand, is anxious about the things of the world, how she may please her husband. I am telling you this for your own benefit, not to impose a restraint upon you, but for the sake of propriety and adherence to the Lord without distraction.

GOSPEL MARK 1:21-28

Then they came to Capernaum, and on the sabbath Jesus entered the synagogue and taught. The people were astonished at his teaching, for he taught them as one having authority and not as the scribes. In their synagogue was a man with an unclean spirit; he cried out, "What have you to do with us, Jesus of Nazareth? Have you come to destroy us? I know who you are—the Holy One of God!"

Jesus rebuked him and said, "Quiet! Come out of him!" The unclean spirit convulsed him and with a loud cry came out of him. All were amazed and asked one another, "What is this? A new teaching with authority. He commands even the unclean spirits and they obey him." His fame spread everywhere throughout the whole region of Galilee.

1ST READING JOB 7:1-4, 6-7

Job spoke, saying:

Is not man's life on earth a drudgery? / Are not his days those of hirelings? /
He is a slave who longs for the shade, / a hireling who waits for his wages. /
So I have been assigned months of misery, / and troubled nights have been
allotted to me. / If in bed I say, "When shall I arise?" /
then the night drags on; / I am filled with restlessness until the dawn. /
My days are swifter than a weaver's shuttle; / they come to an end without hope. /
Remember that my life is like the wind; / I shall not see happiness again.

THE FIFTH SUNDAY IN ORDINARY TIME

PRAISE THE LORD, WHO HEALS THE PSALM BROKENHEARTED 147:1-2, 3-4, 5-6

and the good and gracious award goes to.........
....
....GOD!!!!

who me?!

Praise the LORD, for he is good;
sing praise to our God, for he is gracious;
it is fitting to praise him.
The LORD rebuilds Jerusalem;
the dispersed of Israel he gathers.

He heals the brokenhearted
and binds up their wounds.
He tells the number of the stars;
he calls each by name.

be nice

Great is our Lord and mighty in power;
to his wisdom there is no limit.
The LORD sustains the lowly;
the wicked he casts to the ground.

Brothers and sisters: If I preach the gospel, this is no reason for me to boast, for an obligation has been imposed on me, and woe to me if I do not preach it! If I do so willingly, I have a recompense, but if unwillingly, then I have been entrusted with a stewardship. What then is my recompense? That, when I preach, I offer the gospel free of charge so as not to make full use of my right in the gospel.

Although I am free in regard to all, I have made myself a slave to all so as to win over as many as possible. To the weak I became weak, to win over the weak. I have become all things to all, to save at least some. All this I do for the sake of the gospel, so that I too may have a share in it.

GOSPEL MARK 1:29-39

On leaving the synagogue Jesus entered the house of Simon and Andrew with James and John. Simon's mother-in-law lay sick with a fever. They immediately told him about her. He approached, grasped her hand, and helped her up. Then the fever left her and she waited on them.

When it was evening, after sunset, they brought to him all who were ill or possessed by demons. The whole town was gathered at the door. He cured many who were sick with various diseases, and he drove out many demons, not permitting them to speak because they knew him.

Rising very early before dawn, he left and went off to a deserted place, where he prayed. Simon and those who were with him pursued him and on finding him said, "Everyone is looking for you." He told them, "Let us go on to the nearby villages that I may preach there also. For this purpose have I come." So he went into their synagogues, preaching and driving out demons throughout the whole of Galilee.

The Lord said to Moses and Aaron, "If someone has on his skin a scab or pustule or blotch which appears to be the sore of leprosy, he shall be brought to Aaron, the priest, or to one of the priests among his descendants. If the man is leprous and unclean, the priest shall declare him unclean by reason of the sore on his head.

"The one who bears the sore of leprosy shall keep his garments rent and his head bare, and shall muffle his beard; he shall cry out, 'Unclean, unclean!' As long as the sore is on him he shall declare himself unclean, since he is in fact unclean. He shall dwell apart, making his abode outside the camp." **44–46,**

1ST READING LEVITICUS 13:1–2

PSALM
32:1-2, 5, 11

Blessed is he whose fault is taken away,
whose sin is covered.
Blessed the man to whom the LORD imputes not guilt,
in whose spirit there is no guile.

Then I acknowledged my sin to you,
my guilt I covered not.
I said, "I confess my faults to the LORD,"
and you took away the guilt of my sin.

Be glad in the LORD and rejoice, you just;
exult, all you upright of heart.

♪ I TURN TO YOU, LORD, IN TIME OF TROUBLE, AND YOU FILL ME WITH THE JOY OF SALVATION

2ND READING 1 CORINTHIANS 10:31 - 11:1

Brothers and sisters, Whether you eat or drink, or whatever you do, do everything for the glory of God. Avoid giving offense, whether to the Jews or Greeks or the church of God, just as I try to please everyone in every way, not seeking my own benefit but that of the many, that they may be saved. Be imitators of me, as I am of Christ.

GOSPEL MARK 1:40-45

A leper came to Jesus and kneeling down begged him and said, "If you wish, you can make me clean." Moved with pity, he stretched out his hand, touched him, and said to him, "I do will it. Be made clean." The leprosy left him immediately, and he was made clean. Then, warning the him sternly, he dismissed him at once.

He said to him, "See that you tell no one anything, but go, show yourself to the priest and offer for your cleansing what Moses prescribed; that will be proof for them."

The man went away and began to publicize the whole matter. He spread the report abroad so that it was impossible for Jesus to enter a town openly. He remained outside in deserted places, and people kept coming to him from everywhere.

ACKNOWLEDGEMENTS

CAN YOU FIND THESE GENEROUS DONORS IN THE BOOK?

Kevin Dickinson   Tiffany Dickinson   Gabbi Dickinson   Grace Dickinson

Joseph Dickinson   Ann Marie Dickinson   Elijah Dickinson   Catherine Dickinson

Linda Dickinson   Joe Dickinson   Andrew Adams   Coach TJ Barnes

SPECIAL THANKS TO

All of our Kickstarter Supporters - Without your support, this book would not have been possible.

Travis McAfee - You are an amazing illustrator and an even better friend. We are truly blessed to have you in our life!

Cynthia Stone - You have gone above and beyond in your guidance in navigating the publishing world. You have provided us the peace of mind that is so valuable for first-time authors.

Monsignor David LeSieur - You have been a great spiritual advisor and have helped reigned in some of our wild ideas!

All the priest, leaders, volunteers, and staff at Saint Raphael's in Springdale, Arkansas, and their Children's Liturgy program, which was the launching pad for the concept of the book. - You have all played a large part in helping this concept develop into what it is today.

Startup Junkie - for the initial funding through their business pitch contest.

Martha Paola Bryant - for the cartoon translations for our Spanish version. We hope to expand to other languages to reach children all over the world!

created by kids for kids

The Dickinson family—Gabbi, Grace, Joseph, Ann Marie, Elijah, and Catherine, along with their mom, Tiffany—discuss the scriptures and create drawings to tell the stories. Their dad, Kevin, sends them to Travis, who creates the colorful story panels. Monsignor David, our spiritual director, reviews them, and Mom sends adjustments to Travis.

Once everything is finished, we send all our work to Cynthia Stone at Treaty Oak Publishers. She formats the pages to put this book together and oversees the details to publish it.

ABOUT THE DICKINSON FAMILY

We are a family of 8 who loves our Faith & our Family. When we are not running to and from Sports, Dance and other activities, we love to spend time with each other, our friends and church community.

Gabrielle, 14, is the Business Manager and handles all finances
Grace, 12, is the Director of Sales
Joseph, 11, is the Head Kids Illustrator
Ann Marie, 9, is the Digital Marketing Manager
Elijah, 8, keeps the energy going
Catherine, 5, Well, she's cute and loves Jesus! She has some pretty interesting ideas!

Made in the USA
Coppell, TX
10 December 2020